Rich Inspirations

Promiscuous Poems and Twisted Tales.

by

Richard Palmer

Warning
Contains Adult and Suggestive Material

First Printing: 2016
ISBN 978-0-9525494-9-9

Published by
Anixe Publishing Ltd
77 Ridgeway Avenue
Gravesend, Kent DA12
www.anixepublishing.co.uk

Acknowledgements

I would like to thank my wife Linda for sharing my life and frustrations in producing this book. Without her help, understanding, patience and computer knowledge it would still be a pile of papers.

Thanks also to the members of Paphos Writers Group for help, encouragement and feedback each week.
A special thanks to John Goodwin of Anixe Publishing Ltd. for his help in publishing this book.

Thanks to Martin & Sally Walker, Pauline Jessup, Chris & Sue Scorer, Mike & Rose Caldwell, Kevin & Chris Norrish, David & Carolyn Hart, Peter Bruce & Carole Richards, Ray Flinn & Jaqui Biggs, Brian & Joe May, my lifelong friend Derek Caig, plus many more who have patiently endured my ramblings and given their views often while enjoying a few cool drinks at Yialos Taverna, Coral Bay, Cyprus. Thanks to Pampos, Rena, George and Valentina, owners of Yialos for creating a wonderful setting, inspiring me to write many of the stories.

About the Author

Richard Palmer was born in Stafford UK on 6th, May, 1944. The second eldest of four brothers he lived in Melling, Lancashire, a rural village a mile from Aintree Racecourse, Liverpool, until aged eighteen. He was educated at Maghull Secondary Modern School and Bootle Municipal Technical College, Merseyside. He served for eleven years in the Police force and many years in the motor trade. His writing capabilities began at an early age with short stories, poems and newspaper articles.

After the death of his wife Barbara, aged forty six in 1991, he became a member of Liverpool Writers Club and produced a collection of poems. Years later Rich and new wife Linda ran 'Firkin House', their B& B in Hoylake, Wirral, U K, before retiring to Paphos, Cyprus in 2012. There he is secretary of Paphos Writers Group and Co. Editor of 'The Main Sheet' newsletter at Paphos International Sailing Club.

This book represents past and present material.

CONTENTS

A POEM FROM OUR DOG

No one loves me anymore
No one treats me like a pet
No one bothers to open the door
While I'm outside getting wet
Lots of loving is what I desire
While I'm curled up on the mat
Gently sleeping by the fire
I need stroking and a gentle pat
So next time you visit at my house
love and stroke me like a pet
For if you don't I'll bite your bum
And chew your nuts off you miserable git!

Picture courtesy of **The Stonehouse Inn**,
Michalaki Kyprianou115, Peyia, Cyprus
Tel: +357 26623669 / Mobile 99416397

1

A DATE WITH DESTINY

As I made the phone call I realised that it could totally change my life. My nerves were tingling. I had read the advertisement and knew that there was something different about her, was I stepping out of my league? My call was answered, I spoke with a positive attitude not wanting to show my anxiety, I kept it short, and a meeting was arranged.

For the next two days I could think of nothing else, would we suit each other, could I afford the lifestyle and fit in with her way of life. I was not a classic example of thoroughbred upbringing but if I could adapt, my social standing and image would be highly upgraded and things would never be the same again.

It was a long way to go for a date with destiny. The nerves and anxiety were suddenly forgotten as I saw her looking like everything I had ever dreamed of. Exquisite, graceful, elegant, pure class. I touched her, she did not respond but she did not move away. I touched her again and ran my hands over her body. I slowly removed her top to reveal mouth watering features. There was no resistance apart from a tight fitting strap. I caressed her contours, my heart was pounding, surely very soon I would be inside her. My fingertips trembled with every feel of her sensational body. I felt a vibration, then another. I knew now that she was up for it and ready to go all the way. I entered her and in my excitement I pushed harder, she responded immediately. After a while I gave her as much thrust as I could possibly manage. There was a sudden surge, she gave a little squeal then her juices began to flow away from her.

She began to shake violently, and then lay motionless and silent. I tried desperately to bring her back to life without success. I withdrew from inside her, my body feeling wet. It had been a very momentous day but now the excitement was over. I had been totally elated having had the pleasure of her but now it was a very sad scene. I became extremely emotional and miserable at the thought of having to walk seven miles in the pouring rain to the nearest petrol station.

THE DREAMER

She drove slowly along the narrow dusty road, the pot holed tarmac crumbling at the edges fronting the rows of orange trees, their distinct smell wafting through the open windows of the small hire car. The Cyprus heat and humidity was intense as she breathed in every bit of the slight breeze. Turning the corner, banana plants towered over her on either side, their blue bags giving welcome protection to the ripening fruit. Moving to the entrance of the tavern, a rustic basic building standing alone in flat farmland with the waves of the blue sea and a million sparkling diamonds crashing down onto the rugged volcanic rocks holding it at bay, the never ending horizon looming in the background, a magnificent scene. She was careful not to stir up any dust whilst parking, knowing there were people eating and drinking.

A very attractive woman with a beautiful smile on her rounded face, the dark blonde hair enhancing the deep blue eyes, her figure she thought was not perfect but well developed and she felt good for her age of fifty years.

There were a number of people dining outside the tavern, the inside empty as it was too hot. She chose a quiet spot and settled into a wicker chair after first placing her cushion on it. Looking out to sea among the embracing palms surrounding the tavern she soaked up the peace and tranquility. There was a tingling on her bare foot and looking down found a kitten making itself at home in her discarded flip flops, the kittens mother sitting close by. A fresh mild breeze coming in from the sea, a fishing boat slowly passing by and a cruise liner on the far horizon.

Donning her floppy straw hat and putting on sun reading glasses she became engrossed in her book.

The owner of the tavern Rena, a true friendly Cypriot, enquired in English but with an accent that only Cypriots can do with so much charm and character, whether she would like to eat or perhaps a drink. After ordering a large refreshing "Special Cocktail," garnished with lemon and a peacock fan, she returned to her book. A chapter or so later, stirred by a familiar noise she turned to see half a dozen chickens strutting around followed by a few ducks. Standing up to investigate, she found a menagerie of goats, turkeys, rabbits , pigeons, plus an array of wild birds, mainly sparrows helping themselves to the feed.

The smell of Kleftico and Stifado , the basic dishes of Cyprus cooking in the clay ovens outside, caught her nostrils tempting her to order. Instead, she asked the charming barman, Emanuel to make her another cocktail and Settled down in her new found spot away from the tavern facing out to sea. Her mind began to wander. She sat there dreaming, as a yacht appeared on the beautiful untouched scene and dropped anchor in the bay. The bright orange glow of the sun was becoming lower in the sky; sea birds were magnified as they flew past its deep rich glow.

A man appeared on the deck of the yacht and began waving, she hesitantly waved back. The sun reached the horizon and the yacht was encased in its sphere. Her camera was snapping away to catch this magnificent scene forever. The sun set and the yacht slowly sailed off into the unknown. Sitting there mesmerised by it all and dreaming of sailing away on a yacht with its handsome, rugged owner, she sipped her drink.

The following day after dining outside the tavern and sampling Rena's complimentary homemade chocolate cake, washed down with her new favourite drink, she watched as the yacht appeared and anchored offshore. A dinghy was lowered and the man who had been waving set off towards the tavern. Her heart was racing, her mind now in turmoil and overdrive. All hopes and expectations were dashed as he disappeared from view obscured by the rocks. Time passed slowly and in the heat she fell asleep. A sudden tap on her shoulder swiftly brought her back to her senses although a little bewildered, as standing there was the man from the yacht, masculine, tanned and rugged and in a very charming manner said, 'hello.'

They chatted for an hour and she told him of her dreams, he invited her onto the yacht and there they shared a few more drinks.

'How would you like to spend your life sailing round the Greek Islands,' he asked.

'I would love to' she exclaimed with trembling excitement.

'Meet me at the tavern tomorrow with your possessions.'

'Can't we just go now,' she said with her nerves tingling, no way was she moving off the yacht for a few possessions after an offer like that.

'Fine' he replied, then pulled up the anchor and set sail into the evening light.

'By the way, I forgot to ask your name in all the excitement, I am Costas'.

'I'm Shirley' she replied, 'Shirley Valentine.'

"The Dreamer," was inspired by Pampos, Rena, George, and Valentina, the owners of Yialos Tavern by The Sea, Coral Bay, Pegia, Paphos, Cyprus. Tel: +357 99576980.

PADDLING ALONG

You know I love you; I caress and hold you every night.
You say I turn you on and make your life so bright
But I get no response, you disappear, no reason at all
No explanation! I try to get you back but you don't call
I just get blanked and it's so frustrating
Especially when I am excited and you keep me waiting
Then suddenly you appear, bright and ready to play
I can't get excited as I know you could quickly go away
I slide my hand across you and reach for a vital spot
As I lay on it, my friend, suddenly you are not,
You tell me how your day has been and all the news
Plus the things I could have bought like a pair of shoes
But in my time of desperate crisis when I need you most
you flash your body at me then disappear like a ghost
I am human and have my needs and desires
but in this relationship I think we have crossed wires
You are often very lethargic and don't seem to care a jot
About this on and off relationship you and I have got
So for that simple reason to stop me going mad
I am off to the computer shop to buy a new I-pad.

www.paphoscomputers.com

Tomb of the Kings Road,
Kissonerga
Paphos, Cyprus
Tel: +357 26940841
E.mail dpsltd@cytanet.com.cy

TOGETHERNESS

Glowing embers falling ashes
Fine white wine in crystal glasses
Warm and cosy on the settee
Cuddling close just you and me
Candles flickering music mellow
A string quartet and fine bass cello
I softly kiss and hold you tight
Whispering sweet nothings into the night
Another squeeze a comfort hug
As we gently slide onto the rug
Another wine room now aglow
I think it's time for us to go
Up the stairs and into bed
Nothing else to be said
Out with the light
Are you ready
To fall asleep
My favourite teddy.

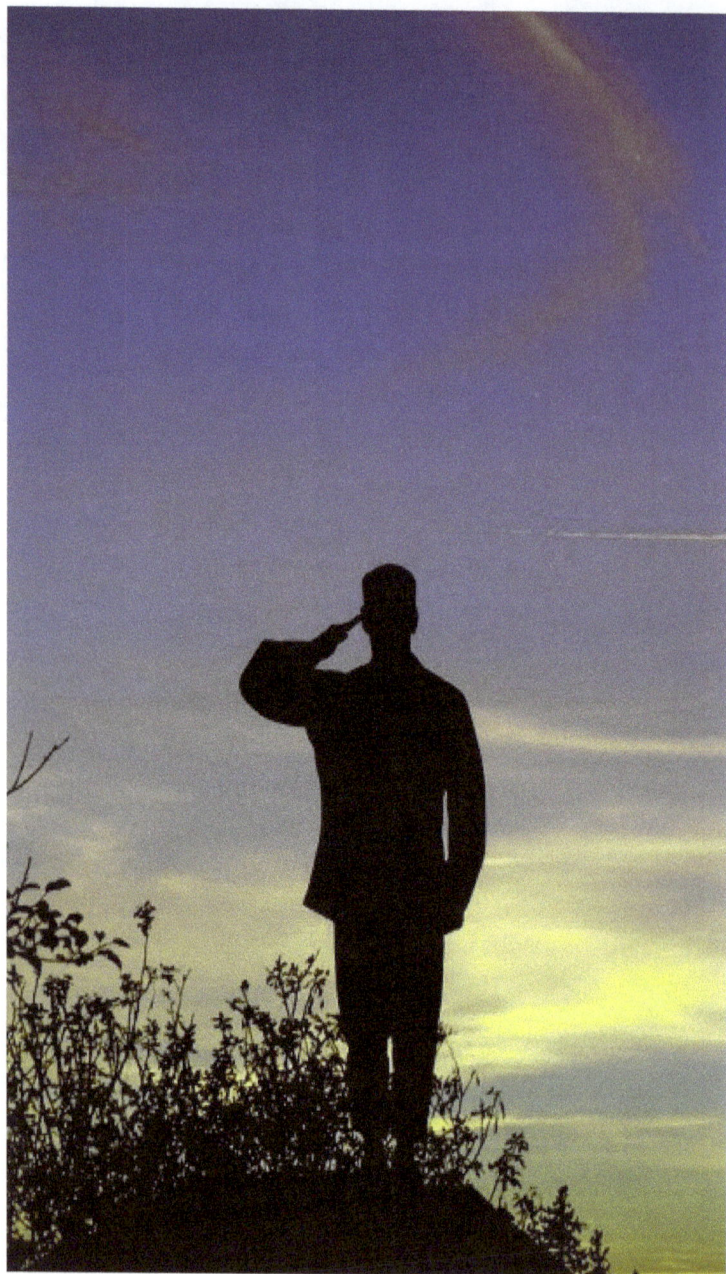

TO LIVE ANOTHER DAY

I don't know the answer I never understood
why people fight each other and shed so much blood
It's not for me to reason I just get the call
To fight another battle and watch the enemy fall
For I am in the military here to do a job
To halt the vicious enemy our lives they wish to rob.
I do not want to fight but it's not for me to say
Just peace on earth will do, that's why
I just want to live another day.
Tomorrow may never come my friends are proof of this
They died in fierce battle a bullet they did not miss.
I am here to fight the enemy to avenge the lives of mates
To live another day before I see those pearly gates.
Peace is all we ask for but peace we cannot make
We must keep on fighting for a town they wish to take.
It's not for me to reason I just get the call
and hope I miss the bullet that would make me fall
So in these times of troubles I hope I have done my bit
to bring some peace to earth before I have to quit.
Loss of limbs would hurt me, its happened to my mates
I will keep on fighting and avoid those pearly gates
For I am in the military, here to do a job
to halt the vicious enemy our lives they wish to rob
I do not want to fight it's not for me to say
just peace on earth will do, that's why
I just want to live another day.

THE WINNER TAKES IT ALL

Bombastic, divorced Peter Delaney was an arrogant sod but he could turn on the charm when it came to women. At forty two he was working as a furniture salesman six days a week. He had grand ideas of owning his own car sales site but without backing that could be difficult. He had a company car and earned a few hundred pounds a week but that soon went on rent for his luxury apartment and his desire to seduce naive women and relieve them of cash.

At work one day, Sandra an extremely attractive elegant slim brunette lady aged about thirty five walked into the showroom. She had an air of sophistication, class and to him, money. She enquired about a new suite, they chatted for a while, she was widowed, he asked her out and she agreed. She explained that her husband, the owner of the largest car showroom in the area had been killed in a car accident and she was left with the worries of the business. Peter Delaneys sinister mind kicked into gear. He wined and dined her, made love to her and swiftly moved into her beautiful detached house with large grounds and indoor swimming pool. There were no children to interrupt his new lifestyle and future plans. He continued with his present job as Sandra's brother had taken over the running of the family business relieving her of the stress. Two years later the brother died of a heart attack, Sandra was distraught. Delaney made his move and persuaded the naive Sandra to let him take over the business. There was a substantial cash flow and he began to splash out on other women, his arrogance reaching new heights. He treated Sandra with contempt and would often stay out all night drinking and womanising. He bragged to his associates, as he had no real friends, of his wealth and female conquests. Most despised him as Sandra was a genuine caring loyal person and they hated what he was doing to her.

A serious recession set in, business began to plummet and the steady cash flow was dwindling. Sandra announced she had serious cancer but he was not interested.

'I need you to take me to the hospital twice a week for treatment' she told him. 'Get a taxi, I'm busy' he retorted. A massive tax bill came in; the business had been evading tax for some years. 'I need money', screamed Delaney. 'Get out, I'm selling up' said Sandra. The business closed and he was forced to move out. Sandra had more important things to deal with like staying alive.

Broke, he moved in with a woman, a part time cleaner, in a rented flat who told him she lived alone but the following month her three kids returned from their father. Sandra made a full recovery, sold the business and her house and retired to live in the sun. A month later she won thirty three million pounds on the lottery. Delaney begged to come back. The naive elegant lady said   xxxx off!

ANDY'S DILEMMA

Andy Jones knew he was capable of achieving better things in life but for now his job in the local supermarket as general dogsbody, cashier and shelf stacker was serving its purpose. The money was low and he had to work long hours to make a decent living and pay the mortgage on the two bedroomed town house he and his wife Maureen had shared for the past five years. Maureen had been involved in a car crash whilst on holiday in Cyprus and received serious injuries to her legs arms and face resulting in a private medical bill of thousands plus the loss of her job as a dental receptionist. It would take a long time for her to recover and in the meantime the bills had been piling up, they were thousands in debt. It was a massive strain on their way of life and they could not see things changing in the near future despite the welcomed benefit payments.

One Saturday night after Maureen had gone to bed Andy decided to stay up and have a couple of drinks as he was not working the following day. He was brooding over their financial circumstances and decided to check the bank account online. It was Maureen's birthday in a couple of weeks and Andy wished he could treat her with a nice present and a lovely day out. The brandy and coke was most welcome but he almost choked on it as he looked at the computer screen, his bank account was in credit, something he had not seen for a long time but it showed they had millions. Andy's heart was racing and his brain was struggling to cope, out of debt, new car, house, holidays, never having to work again. Phone the bank tell them there has been a mistake, he was in a whirl. Another large brandy followed as he weighed up the circumstances. It's their mistake what have we got to lose, a mortgaged house? We will buy one in another country and our family and friends can come and visit us. Should he get Maureen out of bed? No she would try and phone the bank even though it is a bank holiday weekend and they will not be open till Tuesday. Maureen had always lived by honesty but Andy was sick of the stress and strain. He transferred five thousand into one of their other accounts which had ten pounds in it as a result of a Christmas present cheque. As the money went through he shuddered with excitement. Next he tried one hundred and five thousand, it went through. At this stage he knew he could return it but the whole thing overwhelmed him. He tried an account that had been dormant for a few years and transferred five million pounds which also went through. He began to contact friends and family, this continued the next day while Maureen was at her mothers. He told them he had won some money on the lottery and would like to share it with them so they gave their bank details. Money was flowing out of the account in large amounts. He opened as many online accounts as possible and transferred millions. That night he told Maureen that his dad had offered to pay for a week's holiday to Northern Cyprus with spending money.

As they lay on the sun drenched beach Maureen said 'I could stay here forever'. It was then that Andy told her what had happened. 'I don't care anymore do what you want' said Maureen. Andy had no idea who or where the money had come from, there was just some letters and numbers on the statement.

A few days later he received a message to get in touch with his bank which he ignored. Then another message from Europe which he also ignored. Eventually a telephone call from a Mr Doza Bastardo requesting him to please return all monies accidently paid into his account by the I.M.F in Brussels as it is required by Friday at the latest to bail out Greece to the amount of eighty seven billion euro's. 'I apologise if this has been an inconvenience'. Just then the phone battery died. Andy poured another brandy and settling on his sun bed he turned to Maureen and said 'Isn't life just great, do you fancy Greece for a few months?'

THE LOVE OF MY LIFE

We slept together on many nights and as I lay inside her slowly moving up and down in perpetual motion she responded with a gentle quiver and I could feel her whole body in perfect timing with mine. I moved slightly and glanced out of the window, the cloudless night sky with a full moon and billions of stars twinkling away in the never ending atmosphere. Surely life does not get any better than this. I lapped up the whole sensual and magical scene, how lucky was I to have her, so beautiful in every way, fresh and young at only seventeen years.

Only a young man myself at thirty eight over twice her age, but I hoped that if I treated her right and cared for her she would respond and give me years of pleasure and always be there on my travels through life.

I woke the following morning; she was lying very still, looking so peaceful and serene. I smiled at her beauty then straddled my bicycle for the fifteen minute ride towards Coral Bay stopping at a kiosk for milk and the morning paper. The air was fresh the sun was shining and I felt so happy to be alive. We had only been introduced to each other a few weeks ago. I was about to walk into the club in Paphos on a very busy night, she was sat outside looking stunning in the clear night air, I was mesmerised, I had to have her so I made my move. My friends at the club thought I was taking on too much, 'she will be hard to handle, lives in the fast lane and is high maintenance' said one. But I did not care, life is short and an opportunity like this did not come up very often.

We had been out together many times in the past few weeks and most of my friends were really envious which made me feel good. We had a day out to Paphos Harbour and I could feel eyes staring at us. On strolling down the harbour towards the ice cream parlour at the far end close to Paphos Castle I indulged in a triple strawberry flavoured cone, turned to look at her and my drooling increased but not just for the ice cream. Was I over reacting, would I get used to her always being around, I hoped so, our relationship was new and had a long way to go but it was exciting.

A few months later, the feelings were as strong as ever so I decided to throw a party to celebrate our relationship and invited all friends and family to the beach at Agios Georgios. It was a fabulous day with lots of music and dancing, an open bar to get everyone in the mood and a few guests took to the sea for a swim. I stared at her, trembling with the excitement of the day. She was mine all mine and she was the fastest and best looking boat in the harbour.

www.leemarinecyprus.com
Lee Marine
99098596

THE LOVE OF LIVERPOOL

They say it's a bond between the people
could it be the cathedrals one with a squashed steeple
Or the Liver Building with its birds keeping watch
and the Old Customs House is really top notch
Upper Parlie street and the infamous Dingle
A good night out if you are on the pull and single
Wood Street, Seel Street and the Temple Bar
there are loads of clubs, you don't have to walk far
The Albert Dock with its famous yellow duck
it sank once but Scousers didn't give a f...
Fourpence used to buy you a big bag of chips
you could sit on the landing stage watching the ships
The Royal Daffodil and the Iris at their best
sadly no longer, now put to rest
The Empress ships magnificent in style
but long sold off probably cruising the Nile
There are lots of gays and quite a few queens
but Cunard tops them all with fabulous scenes
Liverpool and Everton are the football teams
and the fans red or blue come in streams and streams
whether playing away or at home
they know they will never walk alone
From the Shankly years right up to now
they idolise him and take a bow
Even though he is a Liverpool god
we can not leave out the fabulous Ken Dodd
Cavern Club, Cilla, John, George, Paul and Ringo
plus great nights out at the local bingo

The museums, Tate Gallery and the Philamonic
The Empire, Royal Court, Echo Arena, so symbolic
The Mersey tunnels joining Liverpool to the Wirral
just so Scousers could have a look at a squirrel
There's the Liverpool Echo sent out from Trinity
with all the latest news in the Merseyside vicinity
What is it about Liverpool I really miss
a night out with Scousers taking the piss
The Beehive Mount Pleasant with its rock and roll
The Caernarvon Castle just a short stroll
The banter and humour was simply great
with a bunch of strangers who called you their mate
If you have not had the experience I think it's sad
I have my memories, thank you Liverpool for that I am quite
glad

FRIGHTENING

It was a beautiful cool night, a full moon with millions of bright stars shining down on me, not a cloud in the sky and I was so happy to be alive. The peacefulness was incredible, the air so fresh and the only sound was the odd flutter of a bird resting in the mass of trees and bushes surrounding our home. My partner and family of five were all fast asleep and it was time for me to retire to bed.

The following morning as the sun rose high I stepped outside, the air was no longer fresh and I could smell smoke and burning. My heart began to beat faster for I knew what the smell could mean. I alerted the rest of the family and apart from one who was still coming to terms with waking up we stood outside trying to decide which direction the smell was coming from. Even though there was only a faint hint of breeze it would be enough to drive a bush fire towards us. The strength of the smell increased dramatically as we left our home and hurriedly set off in the opposite direction. Suddenly my partner ran back into our home realising a family member was still inside. There was a deafening crackling sound followed by huge flames and intense heat and smoke, it was extremely frightening. Our home was totally lost in seconds along with a family member and my partner plus my neighbours home with them still inside, scorched beyond recognition.

This was not a time to hang around so we ran ahead of the raging inferno. Eventually, coming to a tunnel we sought sanctuary inside but kept on moving. Emerging from the far end of the tunnel was even more frightening as we were greeted by flames on three sides and the heat was intense. There was no time to take stock of what was happening we just had to run as burning debris crashed to the ground all around us. Our legs were numb but somehow we managed to keep on going. I glanced round at my young family, there were only three, one more had obviously perished. We were now running for our lives, corpses lay around charred beyond recognition and the smell of burnt flesh filled our struggling lungs. I just had to pray that we were going in the right direction. We came to a narrow road and I thought this would be our saviour but no, the tarmac was so hot it was bubbling fiercely so we continued in the bush. This was a living hell, a sudden change of breeze and we would be wiped out. Things were already seriously bad, I had lost my partner, two of my family, my neighbours, my home, it was now a case of coming out alive.

Suddenly a deluge of water appeared behind us followed by another one; I looked up and could see and hear helicopters with their huge water buckets. The sudden rush of water seemed to pick us up and speed us along the hillside, our lungs gasping for air in the thick smoke. Frightening it was not, terrifying was the only word to describe it.

We came to rest in a pool of water clinging to a piece of wood, the flames and heat had subsided to be replaced by dense smoke. It was then I realised there were only two members of the family left with me. The mental strain was unbearable but at least the three of us were still alive. We reached dry land and lay there very weak but glad the frightening nightmare was over.

Eventually we made our way to a relative's home and spent the next few days recovering. I told them it was very scary living in the bush but totally frightening if you are a family of mice. !!

A MONTH IN THE LIFE

Of A Twenty Euro Note

Okay so I am only worth twenty euros, we can't all be born to live with the rich and famous, those people who have bulging wallets with hundred and five hundred notes in them but at the end of the day most of us live the same in a wallet or a safe at the bank. The exception is you will not find them in a cash machine waiting to escape onto the next adventure. My uncle is a five hundred note and all he does is sit in the dark twenty four hours a day praying someone will take him out and show him off, but no one wants him. I on the other hand lead a very busy and interesting life. I get taken to lots of fine restaurants, tavernas hotels and bars, okay sometimes I have to stay in the wallet while the owner pays with the infernal credit card but at least I get to rest. The supermarkets are the worst, I get shoved into a little compartment alongside all the wrinklies and the till is slammed so hard I have a headache for days. Sometimes I am out again in minutes allowing a fifty to take my place while I go to a new adventure.

I was born in two thousand and two so I am quite young to be leading an adventurous life.   My name is M88910335007 but I call myself M007 who spies on people and has lots of interesting escapades. One night I was pulled up from under the floorboards and laid out to rest. I was so relieved to be back in circulation. Suddenly I was pushed into the back pocket of a pair of trousers and we set off on a journey in the car. The next thing I knew I was gasping for air, the bugger had farted, disgusting. We ended up in a posh Casino and as I was pulled out along with others I was dropped and hit the roulette wheel spinning at some crazy speed, well I hardly touched the ground. I was flung across the table and into the crowd of punters. The owner did not even notice I had gone. I landed on the carpet crumpled up and I was severely trampled on more than once. Next thing I knew I was picked up, straightened out, laid over a slot and hit in the middle with a piece of plastic and shoved in a dark hole.

Later it was back to a cash machine, not a good night. I was out again the following day looking a bit rough and was given to a young lad for his birthday. He stared at me then laid me out flat, to my horror he pushed a steam iron over me several times, okay I was free of wrinkles and got a bit of a tan but I was boiling hot, not one of my best experiences. That night I slept under a mattress to keep me looking good and the next day I was paraded around all his family and friends each one running their grubby fingers over me. He passed me onto the owner of the local store who that night went to a strip club and duly placed me in the front of a stripper's G string. Now I am not one to brag but the next time I was in the cash machine I had to tell the others of my experience. Unfortunately for me this stripper also worked part time as a prostitute and was out one night standing under her dimly lit lamp post. A randy bloke came by and gave her a fifty; I got pulled out and was immediately strapped to his excited willy with an elastic band. Suddenly all hell broke loose as I was fiercely pulled back and forth. In a very shaky voice I shouted to the stripper, what's going on? She replied, 'Oh it's a cash in hand job and I'm in a hurry to catch the last bus home'.

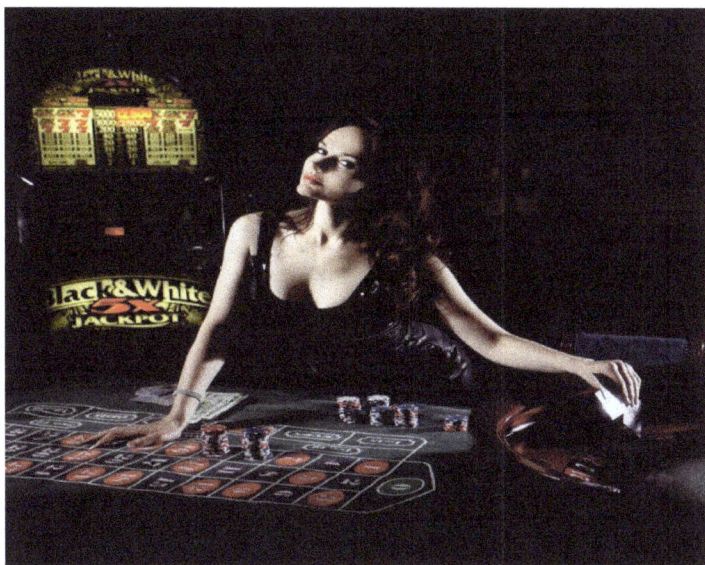

A RESTING DREAM

Intriguing noises, dodgy sounds
from over walls out of bounds
Eerie creaks in the dead of night
so startled was I and in fright
3.00.a.m all should be still
then I spied the open grill
The rear of the bank was insecure
with pumping heart I tried the door
A twist and creak door now ajar
I peered inside but not too far
The dead of silence gently eroding
by a tapping noise so foreboding
A major bank was this my call?
on my feet I could fall
So dark inside crouched on knee
should I stay should I flee?
Thoughts of retiring, oh yes please
heavily perspiring down on my knees
Ten more feet all that is left
to retire on the perfect theft
A sudden rush I was there
money scattered everywhere
I screamed and shouted just stand still
you have just been nicked
By the Old Bill.

THE AIRPORT RUN

The run to the airport is an interesting drive
Down the Tomb of the Kings Road, would I survive
Past the deep blue sea with white foaming waves
crashing on rocks into the caves
A shipwreck to add to the scene,
Making it idylic and so serene
The sun was shining, the air fresh
No chance of cold or feeling nesh
People relaxing in a tavern
Swimmers bathing in a cavern
Restaurants alive with customers having tea
Then a bit further on, a massive JCB

Then another and another plus wagons and tippers
Blocking the paths of the tourist trippers
Roads ripped up, pipes laying bare
But no one around, does anyone care?
Lots of dust and tons of rubble
Surely someone should take the trouble
To sort and tidy this total disaster
Speed up the work, make things go faster
Brake lights on nowhere to go

This crawling traffic is ever so slow
Three years or more it's been like this
The Municipality and contractors taking the piss
Businesses gone bust others struggling to survive
will completion date ever arrive
I blow my horn to no avail
this trip i'm sure is doomed to fail
I reach the island in total frustration
but very short lived is my elation
Traffic is at a standstill in every direction
it's like being at the core of an infection
I check the time, my plane I have missed
If I could move, I would go and get pissed.
A pint or two or maybe a whole bucket
No ! I think instead i'll go in here -

A LIFTING EXPERIENCE

I didn't really want to do this job but on leaving school at fifteen I had no idea what I wanted to do in life or what was expected of me. My mates had their future all mapped out with mundane careers such as bank clerk, shop assistant, bus driver, a few went into the armed forces. The Careers Officer asked me what I would like to do and just for a joke I said bank robber so I can retire early. The thought of working five or six days a week for the next fifty years was daunting but the officer thought I was a bit stupid and was not taking things very seriously. I on the other hand was being deadly serious.

Who says that you have got to work, you only work to support a lifestyle, buy a flash car or a new bicycle in my case. Then buy a house later in life, get married, pay a mortgage for thirty years and bring up a hoard of kids. You would need a lot of money for all that but at fifteen I had no intention of doing any of it, I was very happy living with my mum and dad in a three bedroom semi with my paper round and Saturday cash in hand job at my uncles garage. This gave me enough to pay for my daily needs and the government paid me once a fortnight for doing nothing except visit the job centre now and again to peruse the employment list, none of which I had any intention of taking up.

I continued with this lifestyle for a few years until I met my girlfriend who I thought the world of and decided that she deserved something better in life apart from me. I thought about it long and hard and came to the conclusion that I needed a proper job to keep this relationship going so it was down to the job centre but this time I was taking it seriously. I had read these lists so many times, the same old things, never anything exciting like being a personal assistant to some gorgeous female pop star or helping out on one of those television travel programmes where I would travel around the world. Now let me see, junior chef in a pizza parlour that means a dishwasher on less than minimum wage, junior manager in large supermarket, a shelf stacker on minimum wage, at least we are going in the right direction. What's this? Lift operator required for exclusive casino must be prepared to work shifts and adhere to the ups and downs of the job. Now that sounds interesting and the money is better than most positions plus tips. I drew up a C.V and got my uncle to state that I had been working for him for the past few years as a junior sales manager. I also included four O levels the certificates of which had been destroyed in a house fire recently and as the chosen college which I did not attend had been bulldozed to the ground it was fairly safe to assume that no one would be able to check up. It worked a treat and a week after the interview I started work as a customer care manager otherwise known as a lift operative for this very high class casino. On my first night I was in awe of the plush setting and the wealthy looking punters eagerly placing their chips on the table in anticipation of relieving the casino of some of their cash. I wondered where these people got all this money from, maybe they got a good job when they left school or had a better paper round than me.

I felt a bit envious then thought these people have probably worked six or seven days a week for the last few years, something I had not intended to do. I was shown how to operate the lift and instructed how to deal with the punters pampering to their every whim. After the first week I realised what a brilliant job this was as I chatted away with all the charm of an old pro.

It always made me smile as I read the notice, "Capacity 16 Persons". If sixteen got in I would probably pass out from the fumes of farts from the six people who had polished off a strong chicken curry washed down with a couple of bottles of red wine the night before combined with the smell of cheap perfume and underarm odour from those who got up too late to have a shower. Failing that I would probably get arrested for forcibly being pushed up against the backside of a young girl or worse still a six foot seven seventeen stone man mountain who due to my actions wants to be my special friend forever.

After about six months the job began to get me down as the management who did not care about the staff as long as they were making money began to pile the hours on to such an extent that my love life was suffering as we hardly saw each other. I asked them to take on another operative but they just ignored me. Okay I was making some good money but what use is it if you cannot enjoy it. I began to seriously dislike the management with their non caring attitude and was thinking up crazy ideas to get back at them. Late one Sunday night I was going about my business up down up down but feeling more down than up when two blokes pushed into my lift almost knocking me over and in a threatening manner ordered me to take them to the ground floor, the casino being on the fifth floor. As they threw two large holdalls onto the floor I realised not all was as it should be so on descending I put the lift into the alarm position which caused it to stop between floors. The men now realising that the engineers would soon be sorting the problem out began to panic and demanded that I hide the holdalls on the roof of the lift through the escape hatch and made serious threats as to what would happen to me if I told anyone. I agreed with their demands and eventually descended to the ground floor pretending the engineers had sorted the problem. As the two men got out I swiftly closed the doors and ascended to the next floor again jamming the doors. As a result of a dislike for the management and now seriously having been threatened I decided to pack the job in and left by the fire escape. The following day I heard on the radio that the casino had been robbed by two men.

A week later I took my girlfriend on holiday to Cyprus and as we lay on the beach I asked 'do you fancy staying here forever, we can afford it, and by the way I have given up work and retired'

THE PRISONER

Sealed inside this fortress cell
No air no light a living hell
No smell of grass or sound of spring
No joyful pleasure does it bring
Reinforced to keep me in
but I have committed no act of sin
No sign of ever getting out
No one around to hear me shout
I push and shove to no avail
Heart beating fast, going pale
Rest awhile things turning black
Then it appeared an almighty crack
With racing heart I stood tall
Attacking this crack within the wall
A beam of daylight shining through
To reveal a haze of misty blue
One final push and I am free
A part of life for all to see
With a shake of feathers I now rest
Safely in my parents nest.

A VERY SPECIAL CHRISTMAS

The Christmas holiday period was getting closer and closer, my sister Daisy aged five was a year younger than me and we both were really excited at the thought of Father Christmas his sleigh and reindeers flying through the clear but starry crisp sky on their way to all those chimneys with presents for families to make them very happy. What a lovely man he must be, I would love to meet him one day. I have been to the shopping mall and sat on his knee but I know he is not the real one because there is one in all the big stores. Anyway the real one would be far too busy wrapping presents and making sure his GPS was working properly because he has got a lot of travelling to do in the dark. My dad says the sleigh runs on diesel so it can travel further but my mum tells us not to take any notice of dad, he is just teasing us and anyway everyone knows that his sleigh runs on high octane petrol so he can glide through the sky faster, the problem is it's too deer (sic) to run.

One of the most exciting things is to make our Christmas present lists, dad always says not to ask for too much but we know that Father Christmas is a very rich man, how else would he be able to bring all those presents if he could not afford them. Last year we got everything we asked for but for some reason mum and dad got very little. 'Did Father Christmas run out of presents' I asked my dad. 'No darling, he just did not have a job available for me'. 'You have a good job now what will you ask for this year?' 'Just happiness darling, just happiness'. He gave me and my sister a big hug 'I love you two so much and so does your mum'.

The whole family set about putting the Christmas tree up and making sure the twinkling lights were working properly and all the decorations were in place with the fairy waving her magic wand firmly fixed at the top of the tree. My mum and dad said that if we made a wish the fairy would make it come true. I made a wish that we would always be happy and love each other forever and ever. Dad set the camera up and took a picture of all of us, smiling and hugging each other with the tree twinkling away in the background.

On Christmas day all our family, uncles, aunties and cousins would be visiting after dinner and we really looked forward to that apart from all the sloppy kissing that went on but we put up with it as we got loads more presents and spent a happy time with them all.

The present list had been written and sent to Lapland a couple of weeks ago so all was ready. Christmas Eve came and Mum Dad and Daisy went to visit some friends. I stayed at home too excited to do anything else. Mums best friend Jodie came round to look after me and we sat and watched a comedy film, so funny my sides were aching. I kept looking at the clock as it got closer to bedtime knowing that when I woke in the morning Father Christmas will have been and presents will be at the foot of my bed along with the Christmas stocking full of sweets and other goodies. I got into my nightdress a step nearer the event, curled up on the settee with my teddy bear.

Suddenly there was a knock at the door, Jodie answered it and came back in with a Policeman and woman who told us that my mum, dad and baby sister Daisy had all been killed in a horrific car crash on their way home. I went into hysterics, crying uncontrollably and eventually passed out. When I woke in the morning it was Christmas Day there was not a present on my bed, not a stocking, just a bare room with my teddy bear sitting on a bedside cabinet. My feet rested on a hot water bottle and I tried to warm my cold toes then suddenly I fell back into reality and realised that life would never be the same again now that I was all alone in Dr. Barnardos.

A cold shudder went through my body then I was being shaken and woke to find my mum and dad standing over me saying it was time I was in bed. I burst into tears and hugged them hard.

Merry Christmas!

MY SPECIAL FRIEND

For the past few years I have been living alone
No one to talk to no one to phone
No family or friends no special mate
No one to take me on a romantic date
No one to caress me or hold me tight
No one to make love to during the night
Then one day I remembered a special friend
And decided my sex life I could mend
We lay together on the rug on the floor
Then up the stairs through the bedroom door
Off with my clothes I grasped my friend
And pushed him inside me right to the end
An orgasm was imminent I had no doubt
I screamed as my friend went in and out
Just a few seconds more I cried and cried
Then SHIT ! SHIT ! SHIT !
The battery died.

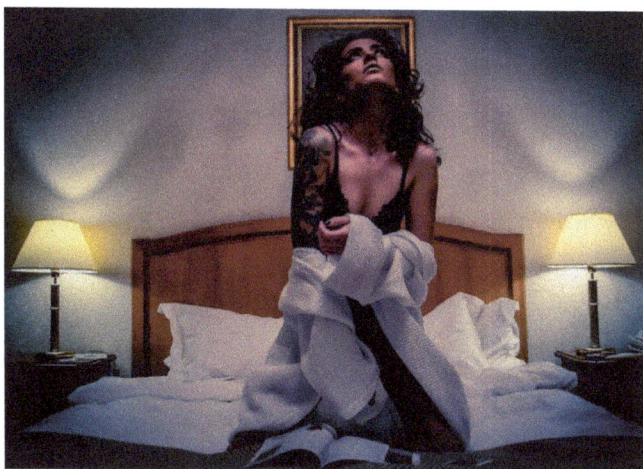

FOREVER FRIENDS

Simon and Terry had been the best of friends since their childhood, attended the same school, in the same class, went on holidays together with their parents. The bond between them was very strong and they had never let anything get in the way of that. Now both aged twenty three the bond was as strong as ever, although Terry lived with the feeling that he was indebted to Simon for saving his life by rescuing him from a burning car at great danger to himself.

Their backgrounds were very different; Simon lived with his parents in a large house overlooking the park in an affluent area. Having obtained three 'A' levels at college he worked in a bank for a while but found it boring and decided to join the Police Force, swiftly becoming a C.I.D officer. Terry was not very academic having left school at the earliest opportunity with an 'F' grade in engineering and moving from job to job the last being in Tesco's as a shelf stacker. Having been arrested for stealing a car he now found himself unemployed and broke. The tension in the terraced house in Birkenhead where he lived with his parents was high due to his circumstances.

Simon wanted the two of them to go on holiday and Terry was feeling guilty at not being able to go. The following day a letter arrived informing him that his uncle had died and left him two thousand pounds. They sat together searching the internet for an adventure holiday and finally booked two weeks in Coral Bay in Cyprus. Simon's parents where already there spending time on their modest yacht. As they left the airport full of excitement and enthusiasm they were met with bright sunshine, intense heat and humidity but it was a welcome change from the miserable weather in the U.K. They settled into their apartment and began to plan the days ahead.

After meeting up with Simon's parents and checking out local attractions for a couple of days, they decided to rent a small motor dinghy and go scuba diving at which they were both experienced. They headed for a remote area and secured the boat before donning scuba equipment. The water was clear, they went down to forty feet amongst the rocks, fish were darting around as they searched through the many different aspects of the coral reef.

Terry decided to be a bit more adventurous and headed into a cave entrance. The beam of his helmet light reflected off something small and shiny and he went deeper to investigate. With a piece of coral safely in his pouch he headed for the surface and in the safety of the boat began chipping away at the lump of coral to find several old coins which appeared to be gold. His heart began to pound, this was seriously exciting. Simon surfaced and he to became excited. Taking tools and net bags, they dived down again to the reef and entered the cave, chipping away at the coral until the nets were full. Back in the boat, they found hundreds of the gold coins, the adrenalin was pumping especially with Terry as he slowly began to realise that his financial problems could soon be greatly eased with their new find.

They took the coins to the apartment and spent a week continuously diving to the reef and brought up a huge amount of coral probably containing thousands of coins.

The small dinghy was not suitable to sit and chip away so Simon's father brought the yacht to within two hundred metres of the reef. Terry and Simon were exhausted and lay back at opposite ends of the dinghy.

Terry's mind raced away with ideas of what he was going to do with all the money from his share. 'I think I will buy a Mercedes convertible' exclaimed Terry with a powerful exuberance.

Simon sat up and was feeling a bit uneasy, he thought Terry was getting a bit carried away by it all. 'They are not our coins' remarked Simon, 'they belong to the state by law, we will have to hand them over to the Cyprus Treasury'. 'Are you mad' shouted Terry, 'finders keepers as far as I am concerned', they would still be at the bottom of the ocean if it was not for us'. 'No matter', replied Simon, 'that's the law of the land'.

Terry was fuming; his anger increasing by the minute, their friendship was in serious danger of cracking up. Simon, being a C.I.D officer, stood his ground much to Terry's annoyance and a shouting match followed as the dinghy set off towards the yacht. Terry felt like punching Simon and throwing him overboard, here was the chance of a new life and he wants to throw it all away. The friendship was crumbling fast as the dinghy got within fifty metres of the yacht. Suddenly a speedboat crashed into them and the two lads were thrown into the sea. The dinghy rapidly sinking with their haul of coins still on board. Terry quickly regained his senses but Simon was not visible. Terry made dive after dive frantically searching for his friend, eventually bringing him to the surface unconscious. He kept his friend afloat with difficulty due to exhaustion until they were rescued and safely on the yacht where Simon eventually recovered.

Back home in Merseyside they continued with their normal lives and a couple of months later, Terry picked Simon up in a gleaming Mercedes convertible. 'You can share it if you like', said Terry. Simon then remembered the first batch of a few hundred coins they had collected, smiled at Terry and replied 'no thanks, I have got everything I want in life, your friendship' and the two sped off laughing out loudly.

THIS LIVING WORLD

I never knew my parents
they died so I could live
They were coloured and very bright
with the happiness they could give
I was found abandoned helpless on the floor
the wind and rain beating down
could I take much more?
Lying in a soggy mire
should I have struggled and hoped?
Battered by life's elements
I was doomed and soaked.
But then a miracle of life came my way
the sun burst through and turned the
gloom into a fine spring day.
I felt energy inside so strong and fierce
I thought my skin was about to pierce
My body grew so strong and tall
never again would I fall
And as for winds and the occasional shower
It did not matter now that I was a flower!

SUPERSTITIOUS! NOT ME.

It had taken Wendy Angela Grimes nearly six months to obtain an interview for a dream job at the highest level of her capabilities and an exceptional salary. Enthusiastic, confident, she was, but with an air of apprehension. The day had to be perfect and she was well aware that it was important to be alert and make sure nothing went wrong. Although not particularly superstitious she did have one thing niggling at the back of her mind, it was Friday the 13th June.

As she rose from her bed, making sure to get out on the same side as she got in, she peered out of a window, the weather looked rather mixed with a rainbow towering over the large oak trees, she stared at its end with beautiful colours and made a wish hoping she would find a pot of gold by the end of the day. She tapped the wooden bedside cabinet three times smiled and went for a shower. Whilst drying off, she heard a commotion outside and on looking through the bathroom window; there were two magpies on next doors roof, squawking away. She turned away but knocked a mirror off a shelf, just managing to catch it as it headed towards the floor. Thank goodness, she sighed, would have been seven years bad luck.

Dressed in a smart grey business suit, she donned a short cape and headed for the train station. Parking the car it was apparent that the cape was inside out, was that a lucky omen or not she mused. While on the platform her mind in turmoil she was aware of a large piece of bird excrement landing on the cape, she was annoyed by the distraction and mess then realised it was a sign of good luck. Just then the station black cat walked towards her and nestled on an ankle, she stroked it gently as it purred away and she smiled, acknowledging its presence. Stepping off the train and onto the high street her right palm hot and itchy, she saw an unusual sight, a chimney sweep gathering his tools from the back of a van, she smiled again. After a short distance she became aware of not stepping onto the lines of the flagged pavement, then came across a pound coin lying across one of the lines tails up. She stopped to pick it up then remembered and reluctantly left it where it was and continued on. A ladder blocked the path causing her to walk around it just as a concrete block fell from the roof under the ladder, she smiled.

On entering the impressive office building, the automatic doors opened welcoming her presence. The lift to the first floor was out of order so she took the stairs, thankful no one was coming down them. Ushered into a large elegant office the door displaying a brass plaque engraved General Manager she was bemused by his antics as he opened up a large brightly coloured golf umbrella, " came in the post this morning" he explained, folding it down but unfortunately knocking a mirror off his lavish large mahogany desk, shattering on the floor. "Oops, seven years bad luck there" he exclaimed.

The interview over Wendy returned home.

A week later she was recalled to the office to be told the job she had applied for had been taken but would she like the General Managers position.

Her heart fluttered with excitement, this was far greater than she could ever have dreamed of. 'What happened to the general manager?' she asked,' Oh very sad but he walked under a ladder and onto the side of the road in the high street and got hit by a chimney sweep van and died.

HAPPY BIRTHDAY

Another birthday it's a crying shame
I'm too old to be on the game
I'll miss the lamp post with its dim light
And all my customers throughout the night,
There's Peter, Joe, Fred and Dick
And some big bloke who's a total
Pricked my finger late last night
It turned blue and my face turned white
A customer said are you a ghost?
Then walked into my dimly lit post
Another birthday it's a crying shame
I'll miss my friends whilst on the game
Four quid a night is what I made
As sixteen blokes I happily laid
The sex was fantastic for a one night stand
Romping around on fertile ground
Flapping limbs, legs akimbo
We even did it while doing the limbo
But another birthday it's a crying shame
I'm now too old to be on the game
I'll have to stick to just one bloke
And pray I'll get the occasional poke
But then there's Richard, Noel and Dave
I'll always give them the occasional wave
And if in my car I'll give a honk
And suggest a good old fashion bonk
No longer living in the fast lane
I'm now too old to be on the game
Another birthday it's a crying shame

THE LIFE OF JOHN SMITH

My life was okay, nothing special, just okay. I had enough money for my lifestyle, a decent car, my own house paid for, the occasional exciting holiday in Skegness staying at a four star hotel overlooking the murky sea, okay when the sun was shining, a bit grim when it was not, but I just liked the place. Some fine old buildings and architecture, the solace of my hotel room and the hustle and bustle of the tourists checking out the town and its attractions.

Just an escape from my life as an accountant with a large insurance company based in the Royal Liver Building Liverpool. A fine city with its very friendly people, superb architecture like the three graces consisting of the Royal Liver, The Customs House and the Port of Liverpool building. Others include the Tate Gallery and museum complimented by the new Echo Arena attracting top artists from around the world. I suppose I should be grateful for being part of it all but working in a large office five days a week with the lights on to make up for the lack of daylight, especially in the winter, was not the most glamorous job in the world and the prospect of promotion was almost non-existent unless someone died.

Whilst lying in bed one night after a few large brandies, I began to sum up my life and thought, how predictable and mundane, I was still fairly young at fifty three, secure but bored, I needed a drastic change. My wife had been killed in a car accident a few years earlier so I had no one to share with, I could do whatever I wanted.

Leaping out of bed I poured another large brandy then went into the lounge and began to write down all the things I would like to do similar to a bucket list of twenty things to do before you die, but being only fifty three that number may have to be increased. Topics included, a flight down the Grand Canyon, a visit to Australia and the Sydney Opera House, Thailand and the Far East, the Hawaiian Islands and Honolulu, an African Safari, a hot air balloon trip over the Amazon river and forests.

Over the following week, I completed the list of twenty, my mind was now made up, I was determined to enhance my life and chose a balloon trip over the Amazon. I booked three weeks off work and arranged for the trip in a month's time. My head was buzzing, I had never done anything this exciting in my life, Skegness had disappeared to the back of my mind.

Over the next few weeks I sorted out everything I would need for the trip, passport, injections, suitable clothing and even treated myself to a new camera with a powerful zoom lens to snap scenes I would not normally get with my old camera.

The day of adventure duly arrived and in the humid searing heat on an open plain in the Amazon jungle I stepped into the basket and looked up at the huge red and white balloon towering overhead, the burners blasting flames skyward to fill it with enough hot air to lift it off the ground, an amazing sight. Except for the pilot, this was a solo flight, I wanted to soak up the whole atmosphere without the interruption of others. A few more blasts and the balloon slowly lifted skyward, my heart was pumping, the adrenalin and excitement coupled with unknown expectation was totally exhilarating, higher and higher it soared, the views were unimaginable, my new camera snapping away to save these incredible scenes forever.

After about thirty minutes the burners began to splutter, the balloon was losing height, the pilot desperately trying to make them function, but to no avail. I watched terrified as the basket was about to hit the tree tops, the wind urging it sideways at what seemed like a hundred miles per hour. I cowered at the bottom of the basket, rolled in a ball, the noise was deafening as the basket crashed from tree to tree, I was buffeted all around, there was a tremendous thud and my whole body was dashed against the side of the basket. As I opened my eyes it appeared dark then a faint beam of light made me squint, I sought to collect my senses, checking my aching body and was relieved to find I had no broken bones. The basket was lying at an angle stuck in the branches of the Amazon jungle. The pilot had been thrown out and I was left to free myself in a dazed and badly bruised state. After a while and much difficulty I managed to reach the ground, the pilot was dead, I was alone. The heat and humidity together with the smell of rotting vegetation was almost unbearable but I did have a food and survival pack from the basket.

Which way do I go, it was so dense even the stars could not be seen. I calculated the course of the balloon and the time we had been out then headed in the hopefully appropriate direction. The going was slow and difficult and my aching body did not help but after a week or so my food and drink had run out, I was exhausted beyond belief. I lay against a tree and decided this is where I was going to die. The noises of the jungle, birds, animals, insects, numbed my brain, my throat had dried and I was having trouble breathing. I woke to find I had been there for hours, a little refreshed for my rest and sleep. Suddenly, I heard a noise in the distance of an engine running. I pulled myself to my feet and slowly headed in the direction of the noise. Sometime later I stumbled onto a clearing to find it bare, my hopes faded, I was sure the noise which had now stopped had come from this direction. To my total jubilation I heard the noise again and as I lay totally exhausted on the ground, a helicopter appeared encased in bright sunshine above the Amazon trees.

Back in Liverpool and fully recovered from my ordeal, I reflected on my terrifying experience and my life as an Accountant, with my moderate house and car, secure in the knowledge that I worked in the Liver Building, one of the most iconic buildings in the world where I was safe and had a good stable life which I was now thankful for. I picked up my bucket list and slowly read each life changing event, they were certainly exciting, I spoke into the phone, I would like to book a trip please. I felt happy and at ease knowing that very soon I would be spending two glorious weeks in SKEGNESS !!!.

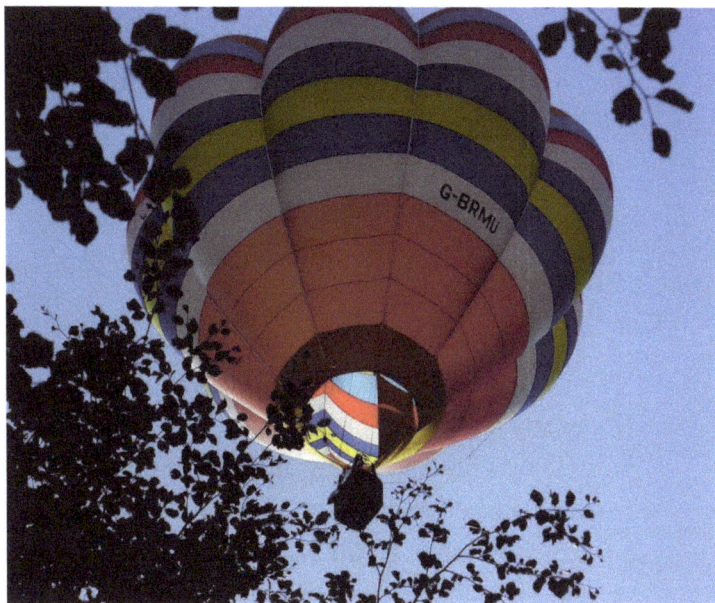

LOST FOREVER

I've lost it! I've lost it!
Oh what an awful plight
I know I had it when I went out last night
Handbag in tow, hair all done
with a cute sexy dress just covering my bum
Sweet sixteen and dressed to thrill
a whole nights clubbing yet to fill
A black lace thong and matching tights
to excite the lads on warm summer nights
Four inch heels, boobs on show
I was ready to Go! Go! Go!
A load of booze head all fuzzy
I vaguely remember the twang of my sussy
He was big and strong and very tall
as he pushed me up a rough brick wall
From then on all went black
and I remember nothing till I got back
I woke in the morning and searched far and wide
but I could not find it and that hurt my pride
I've lost it! I've lost it! Oh where can it be?
I'll go back to town and maybe, just maybe
I searched far and wide in the vicinity
But I never found my precious virginity.

MY SUPER HERO

Jimmy Webb was born a normal boy who played with his mates and did all the exciting things that young boys do. He went to an ordinary school and was quite bright and enjoyed the activities especially sport as he dreamt of being a footballer. Sadly his dream ended when at ten years old he was diagnosed with a brain dysfunction which left him with speech and learning difficulties plus a slight limp. As a result he was taken away from his school and friends to be placed in a special school which catered for his problems.

He lived with his mother and father, an older brother and eight year old sister in a three bedroom flat in a high rise block on the outskirts of a bustling city. Poverty was rife and there were a lot of people in need of help. When he was old enough he worked on a paper round with a local newsagent which included two high rise blocks and a row of shops. It gave him some independence and the chance to meet and help people who were mainly old and not in a position to do some things for themselves. There were problems such as the lift breaking down from time to time and he had to struggle up the twenty plus flights of stairs with his bag laden with newspapers and magazines. The money was not great but it allowed him to buy a brand new top of the range Playstation which was his lifeline and he spent hours on it.

His hero was Spiderman and he was totally convinced that he was a real life super hero and no one on the planet could ever tell him any different, he lived in a Spiderman world. He had the full red and blue spider suit with a battery operated web blaster which sent out a powerful cord coated with a strong sticky substance. He daydreamed of flying through the air between the high rise blocks tossing his papers on the way. He had no fear of danger and believed he could do anything his super hero could do. His mother spent a lot of time trying to convince him that his hero was not real and she did not believe in superheroes but he was having none of it and Spiderman was his friend. He liked to think that while he was doing his round he was on a mission and readily available for any emergencies that may arise just like his super hero. Over the next year he had to deal with quite a few of these tasks much to his delight. There was the blind old lady in flat fourteen who totally relied on her portable radio, just like Jimmy's Playstation the radio was her lifeline to the world. Some scumbag had stolen it when she answered the door. The same day Jimmy turned up with a replacement from the charity shop and tuned it in. Another lady who was not good on her legs also received some of Jimmy's kind treatment when he took her sick cat to the vets and on his return he brought her shopping back. Word soon got round that Jimmy was helping out and he began dog walking, cleaning, painting, making meals and sitting having a cup of tea with lonely people who began to look forward to his visits.

He supplied some second hand televisions and heaters for the cold winter nights, much appreciated by the residents suffering from arthritis and other ailments. On another occasion a man known to him had to get to a chemist urgently for his aging fathers' medicines so Jimmy gave him the use of his bike and continued with his round on foot.

Christmas was fast approaching, a happy festive time for a lot of people but the winter weather had already set in causing more hardship.

He began to make up food parcels in his mums kitchen but made sure she or the rest of the family were out. It's not that she would be against it but the family were not very well off and had struggles of their own at times.

Despite all his kindness and good deeds he did have a strange outlook when it came to pets. He loved to play with them, chase them round the room or down the street, he meant no harm but would let loose with his web zapper resulting in the family cat or next doors dog being bound up so much that they had to be carted off to the vet to be untangled. The family cockatoo did not escape his pranks and was zapped in mid flight across the living room resulting in a dive straight into the back end of the sleeping cat on the settee which loudly farted in sheer fright and put the Cockatoo in a deep coma for hours which was fortunate for the vet who had to sort out the sticky mess.

One day Jimmy was chasing the cat around his bedroom, the cat realising what was about to happen leapt out of a window that had been left open. Jimmy ran and fired his zapper but in his excitement tripped and fell out of the window three floors up. He was pronounced dead at the scene and the local community began to realise what a great asset he had been and how much he would be missed. The funeral took place several days later and family plus hundreds of Jimmy's friends turned up to pay their respects to a young lad who had helped so many people. He had a belief which so many scorned including his family but it gave him a lot of satisfaction. The mourners left leaving his mother standing alone reminiscing about the life of her young son and his beliefs. Suddenly a strange figure appeared at her side and laid a hand on her shoulder in a comfort gesture. He stared at the gravestone and read out the epitaph from his mother. Here lies Jimmy Webb 'a true superhero.'

The stranger silently disappeared into the distance leaving her to her thoughts. She placed a hand on her shoulder where he had comforted her and felt a strong sticky substance, the smell of which she had known many times.

FIRST LOVE

Rebecca was ten years old when they first met and even at that tender age it was love at first sight. Harry was gorgeous with big brown eyes and a happy smiling face, she could not resist him.

Each day after school he would be waiting for her, ready to give lots of affection. They would spend hours together sharing personal intimate thoughts that she would not dare tell anyone else. She knew he was a good listener as he never interrupted while she was pouring her heart out. She felt very privileged to have someone like Harry and loved cuddling up to him while listening to her favourite music. As she grew older Harry was still there for her and would go on holidays with the family, she could not bear to be parted from him.

As the years passed Rebecca grew into a beautiful young woman and worked in the city meeting lots of new people, eventually dating a handsome young man from the office called Patrick and they shared many tender moments together. One night after a romantic dinner and a few drinks, Patrick and Rebecca retired to the bedroom. Harry lay on one side snuggled up to Rebecca while Patrick made passionate love to her. After about ten minutes at the height of passion Patrick became uneasy and got out of bed. 'What's the problem? ' enquired Rebecca, 'I can't do this with him in bed next to you it does not feel right.' 'Where I go Harry goes' she remarked. 'Well I have had enough' said Patrick and with that left slamming the door on his way out.

Rebecca returned to the bedroom, smiled at Harry lying relaxed on her pillow. She got into bed, kissed him and gave him a cuddle and thought, don't know what's up with him, lots of girls take their teddy bear to bed with them.

MORNING GLORY

An eerie silence from the cold fresh morning
frost on the window in a background of fog
As I awake in my bedroom gently yawning
where I slept the night like a log
The trees hanging heavy from the morning dew
no wind or sun or hint of rain
Not a bird in sight or sound of a coo
as I gaze out through the window pane
Total stillness, nature silent and pure
I move not a muscle to spoil
As I soak up nature totally raw
waiting for life to uncoil
But the silence was suddenly shattered
as this beautiful scene fell apart
For the only thing that mattered
was my stupendous fart !!!

Thanks to our great friends Martin and Sally Walker
Of Oakworth, Keighley, Yorkshire for inspiration
while staying at their home.

TEA TIME

Once again it was tea time with the family around the old oak dining table, the candle lamps barely giving enough light to see what you are about to eat. The thick old stone walls of the house tucked away in a tiny hamlet in the country, gave no warmth to the occasion except for the fresh damp logs placed on the open fire in an attempt to raise the blood circulation on this cold winters evening. Frozen snow glistened in the light of the moon as an owl hooted from a nearby tree struggling to hunt down prey in such conditions. Old blankets and sacks hung over doors and windows in an attempt to keep out the howling wind, while the family wore many clothes including overcoats. It had been a long hard winter and food had been in short supply apart from eggs courtesy of the chickens and pork from the few pigs they kept on the small piece of ground at the rear of the house.

It was sixteen seventy two, a harsh time for a growing family with very little prospect of improvement, having to live off the small plot and do any odd jobs that came their way. As the mother placed the food on the table as she did every evening, the son now sixteen burst into a tirade of verbal complaining and whinging about having to eat the same thing night after night. It was not his mothers fault, she had always worked hard and done her best for him and his fifteen year old sister. 'I am fed up with pork belly night after night, it makes me sick', he cried. 'Well if you don't like it, do something about it' said his mother in frustration as his father sat there silent, unable to work due to chronic arthritis. The following morning as the family sat round for breakfast, there was no sign of the son, his bedroom was empty, his clothes and rucksack gone, all that was left was a trail of footprints in the frozen snow. The family were upset not knowing where he had gone or what had happened to him, there was no contact and they were left to carry on with their everyday lives.

Ten years later there was a knock on the door and as the mother opened it she barely recognised the smart handsome man in uniform as her long lost son. She hugged him fiercely as they went inside. Just as the family were preparing for tea he threw some bags on the kitchen floor. 'What have you got there son?' asked his mother. 'It's Sir if you don't mind Ma' pulling her leg. 'Well, if you are a Sir young man, you can call me Mrs Raleigh and are you having pork belly for tea?' 'No Ma, sorry Mrs Raleigh, I am going outside for a smoke of my new tobacco and I will have egg and chips for tea, the spuds are in the bag.' 'That's fine Walter, welcome home son.'

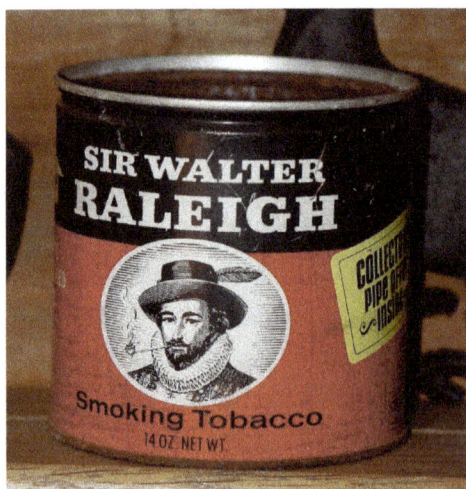

THIS LIVING WORLD

I was created from another,
an offspring brought into this living world
I had been slowly growing with my mother
firmly attached inside a darkened home.
Members of my family were all around.
I became detached, parted from my family and
placed in a new home, but this was also
dark and I was so alone.
Trapped inside this cold dark tomb
I fought to free myself in an effort to enter a
brighter and more interesting life.
I pushed myself hard determined to reach my goal
and after months of perseverance I was
greatly rewarded one fine spring day.
The air was fresh, the sun was shining
a new life had just begun.
As time passed I grew more beautiful each day
and people would stop and stare at me whilst
passing extremely flattering remarks such as
How beautiful! Absolutely gorgeous!
They would give me lots to drink and I would
bask in the sunshine until sunset, when I would
look back on the day and life itself and think
It was tough being a bulb
but it's great being
A FLOWER.

THE SCARIEST MOMENT OF MY LIFE

It was a beautiful sunny afternoon in the summer of fifty two
no school that day so serene no one to tell me what to do
but where to go where to play or maybe some other
In the end I stayed at home with my younger brother
I was eight he was four I held his hand, we went out of the door
down the garden right to the bottom
Little did I know this would be a day never to be forgotten

Into the sand pit we both sat ,followed by Lucky our tabby cat
I dug a hole a foot or so wide and with my legs I stood astride
Then head down arms tucked in I entered the hole deep within
Very soon things went black then I knew I could not get back
Fear and panic suddenly set in, I realised things were very grim

Eight years old I was far too young to die
Then emotion took over and I began to cry
Never again would I see the light of day
Never again would I go out to play
Never again would I see my brother
Or hug and kiss my lovely mother

Sand in my mouth and eyes, I let out a series of desperate cries
"Fetch my dad," I screamed at bro, I didn't really want him to go
To be alone, a serious fear then I felt something move by my ear
The sand fell to the ground, all I could hear was a clawing sound
I was free to breath in the air, all I could feel the nuzzle of fur
I moved my head and upright sat laughing at the sight of our cat

he was covered in sand but saved me from hell
as he clawed and clawed to the sound of his bell
he was a cat like no other then
I burst into tears at the sight of my brother.

THE DREADED WEED

I live in a packet on a shelf
I'm there for everyone including yourself
Part with the money and I will be yours
I will calm your nerves when we are indoors.
Light me up flick my ash
you will puff and squeeze me in a flash.
Take out another a friend of mine
light him up when you go out to dine
Now you have smoked you feel sane
but don't forget we will affect your brain
Twenty a day, you will find the need
to give up this wacky addictive weed
Mouth like a sewer, health in decline
but another fag and you feel fine,
Give up ! Give up! Before it's too late
or you will soon be outside St. Peter's gate
Nerves are gone, life's a drag
you have got to have another fag
You reach for the packet so full of sorrow
Oh stuff it all I'll give up tomorrow!

SCREWED UP

Peter Jones paced around his large eighteenth floor corporate office in the centre of Manchester, a soft gentle lullaby was playing on the radio, easing the turmoil in his mind. He stopped to stir his morning coffee to find there wasn't a spoon, could things get any worse. He opened the office door adorned with horseshoes for good luck and found one hanging loose. No wonder things are going wrong, he screamed at his secretary, "Mary, the horseshoe needs a screw ". He reached over and removed her stained teaspoon from the saucer on her desk. He took no pleasure in shouting at Mary but he had asked her to sort the horseshoe out for weeks and now his nerves were at breaking point.

That morning he had to make an agonising decision, take early retirement and a redundancy payment or move to new offices in London. The board considered that he had brought disrespect and disgrace to the company by having an affair with a married female member of the staff. Peter thought the board of directors decision to relocate him was atrocious. Should he stand and fight, it felt like war. He entered the boardroom, the silence numbing his brain, it was over in minutes. He returned to his office, cleared his desk, picked up his umbrella and slammed the door on his way out. A clanging sound was heard; he looked round to find a horseshoe spinning on the floor. He turned to face his secretary, Mary and said, 'Next time you are asked to screw something, make sure it is not your boss!

MY FAVOURITE BOOK

It was a beautiful summers day in the leafy tree lined village were the main character of my favourite book lived. He was very well known locally for his flamboyant style of dress and had built up a bit of a reputation for breaking the rules especially when it came to his driving ability. He managed to get into a bit of bother with the local Police on several occasions for illegal parking or speeding which he had a habit of doing. Usually he got off with a caution being well known and living in a small community but he knew he would have to change his ways otherwise he could lose his licence and that would cause him many problems.

He enjoyed driving around in his classy convertible with its personal number plate; it was a real eye catcher and attracted a lot of attention. His close friends sought his company in order to share the car with him and that is when he would show off and get into trouble.

He was a smart looking chap and owned a nice house in the village. On several occasions he fancied some female company and placed an advert in the local paper which read 'flamboyant young man smart appearance own house and car wishes to meet interesting female. Unfortunately none of the females he met wanted to see him again, whether it was his mode of dress, lack of sense of humour, too flamboyant or they were put off by the portly teddy bear on the back seat, he did not know. I always liked to read about all the scrapes he got into not knowing what was coming next. He thought he led an exciting life which females would enjoy and find interesting but it was obviously going to take a very special person for after all it is not every females ambition in life to date and go out with NODDY!

THE ULTIMATE SACRIFICE

Irish lad Paddy O'Donnell had a tough upbringing in his hometown of Dublin in Northern Ireland where he had lived with his parents Pat and Mick. His brother Paddywack was half Irish and half Scouse, due to his father attending a stag weekend in Liverpool ending up in an entry at the rear of the Grafton Ballroom with a lady of ill repute who only looked good after fifteen pints of Guinness. After three minutes and ten seconds the deed was done which was surprising as apparently it took him three minutes to drop his trousers. I do not think there was any love or passion involved, it started with him wrapping a ten pound note to his willy as she demanded cash in hand. From then on it was a case of stagger, aim, fire!

When Paddywack was about five, he asked his mother one of those awkward child questions, 'Mum, do you have to pay for babies?'

His mother replied, 'Not normally son but your dad made an exception in your case, he said it was worth every penny.'

Paddy's family were quite poor, mainly due to his father coming home legless each night having spent most of the wages he earned as a cleaner at the local brewery. Paddy struggled at school but was determined to lead a better life than his parents.

When he was eighteen Paddy and his family moved to the outskirts of London in a rented house supplied by the government. His father was now a full time carer for his mother who suffered from dementia. Paddy did a few mundane jobs before becoming a Financial Advisor at the age of twenty. He soon made a name for himself and built up a reputation of being a high flyer. He had the drive and determination to succeed and his love and passion for hitting targets became the talk of the office. He wallowed in the emotions of the business world, the intense pressure, stress and strain on the nerves and the immense effort required to be the best.

Paddy was lacking academically but brilliant at figures. After a couple of years he was head hunted by a rival company and given a high salary with a powerful luxury car and generous expenses. He continued to excel with life in the fast lane, by this time he had moved away from his family and was living with his girlfriend, a law graduate and junior lawyer, in an upmarket apartment in the city centre. They mixed with the financial elite set where Paddy's reputation was well known. Their social diary was constantly full but Paddy always found time to visit his family.

After a couple of years, his drive, manner and passion for success began to affect him and he found he wanted more and more. At a social gathering in Chelsea one night Paddy was given the details of a financial position in Sydney Australia with an unbelievable salary plus company shares, car and expenses. The following morning he phoned and was accepted for an interview locally.

There were four people in the interview room but they were interviewing all day for the next three days. Paddy was confident due to his track record but at the back of his mind was the thought of his lack of general education. The interview over, he came out feeling positive. At this stage he had not discussed the proposition with his partner as although he was confident he knew he was up against high flyers with an Oxford or Cambridge education. He would wait and see how far he got.

A second interview came a week later, then a third. A few days later Paddy received a letter informing him he was one of two remaining candidates for the position but the final interview would be in Sydney and all expenses would be paid. His mind was now in turmoil, he would have to discuss it with his partner. Things did not go well, she was adamant that she was staying put due to her career and friends and thought Paddy was mad to ask her to give it all up. He fought with the decision all week and a few days later he set off for Sydney. He had bought a very expensive suit and shoes just for the interview. The day before leaving he received a message to say his mother was dying and would he return home immediately. He wrestled with his conscience but decided to go on.

The day of the interview arrived and he entered the plush offices overlooking the sea in a very affluent area. A few minutes in the lift took him to the twentieth floor. He hoped his passion for figures was about to pay off.

After the interview a written test of twenty general questions was taken by the two candidates. Paddy sat nervously in the interview room, this job was like winning the lottery, his life would be transformed. The other candidate was a Rumanian whose English was not too good and his dress sense was something to be desired. Paddy, said the interviewer, you both have impeccable track records and you both got nineteen questions right, but we have to give the job to the other candidate. But I am British and speak perfect English so why should he get the job? Because we need integrity and honesty. On question fourteen he wrote, "I do not understand this question," and you wrote, "Nor do I."

Sadly, on his return home there was no passion, no integrity, no girlfriend and no mother, she had passed away without him saying goodbye.

NO SIDE

In 1875 the mere thought of my existence was one of pure fantasy. There were many who would have liked to have given birth to me but eventually after numerous attempts I was born on 5th September 1879. It was a very difficult and delicate birth as I was so weak and feeble no one expected me to live very long. My family who had conceived me nervously sat around praying I would survive. Suddenly I burst into life and their faces lit up with excitement from the previous doom and gloom. I had arrived and although I did not know it at the time, I was destined for great things and over the years I would change the world for the better.

As time passed I grew stronger and stronger and became very famous, people around the world sought for my presence and were astonished by my powers. I was sent to a highly acclaimed school and the teachers bounded with excitement and enthusiasm at my inclusion, their faces glowed knowing my existence would change their lives forever.

Over the next few years I became a great success and went on to win many awards. After my school period I travelled a lot and became very well known around the world. I was in demand in England and throughout Europe but eventually all this was taking its toll and I was unable to cope with my daily routine. People became very demanding of me and I was forced to have a delicate operation which involved inserting a steel plate inside me. I was not happy but I came out stronger much to the delight of my fans. I was constantly being quoted in newspapers and on the radio as one of the greatest and brightest discoveries of modern times. I was flattered of course but merely doing my job. I was highly charged and switched on and was expected to raise my standards all the time with the intention of making people's lives more comfortable and enjoyable. I was present at many emergencies and helped save the lives of many people. In various parts of the world I worked shifts which meant I slept during the day but was expected to be bright and alert during the night. This was obviously tiring and drained my strength slowly reducing my life span. Other positions I had resulted in me working in a large multi story office during the day allowing me to sleep normally at night except for emergencies; this was a far better way of life.

By 1979 I was old and people no longer required my services and over the next few years I was replaced by more sophisticated types, I became obsolete and died.

Since then the world has continued to progress without me and has been led into a more promising direction allowing everyone to have a brighter future.

You may believe this story or think that I was merely a filament of your imagination.

No side = Edison

RETIREMENT

The flickering candles melting like tears
remind you of your passing years
First shining brightly full of fire
lots of glow and burning desire
A golden flame ever so bright
strong from the dawn into the night
But time ebbs by and erodes away
memories of a distant day.
Life goes on so be content
now you have reached retirement
Burning ambitions can be released
as working years have pleasantly ceased.
So congratulations and many cheers
Good luck and best wishes
In your retirement years.

THE COMMUTER

Rick woke around 3.0 am and wiped the sleep from his weary eyes. The comfort of his bed with soft cotton pillows complimented with a blue and white duvet made it difficult for him to leave his warm haven of rest. The central heating and the harsh icy weather added to his annoying but minor dilemma. Being a thirty year old graduate high flyer for one of the largest corporations in London meant that he was required to spring into action. He had carried out some business dealings the day before which niggled at the back of his mind. He was not sure that he had taken the right course and wanted to correct things before the office opened for business, so it was very important that he was not late. He swung his lean athletic body out of bed and headed for the bathroom in his Victorian two bed roomed flat in a peaceful village on the outskirts of the Yorkshire moors. A long way from London but Rick preferred the countryside with its beautiful scenery and tranquillity away from the fast pace of life the hub of city commerce created.

The hot shower steamed up the windows with their cold exterior forcing Rick to wipe them with a soft towel before continuing to shave and put on his business suit with white shirt and appropriate tie followed by gold cufflinks. With a final brush of hair, he donned his patent leather shoes, picked up his briefcase and keys and stepped into the crisp morning air. For a moment he stared at the vast amount of stars in the universe before realising how cold it was as his body gave a gentle shiver. He closed the automatic garage door, the B.M.W black leather seat cold to his warm body causing another slight shiver as he started the engine and left the garage. The heater was swiftly turned to heat mode and with the added luxury of heated seats he soon warmed up as the car roared off into the darkness of the morning.

He had been working on the second floor of the old prestigious building for two years and the place was a hive of commercial activity with a large amount of staff fervently going about their duties. He commuted there in the early hours of a Monday morning returning late on Friday evening giving him two days to relax and unwind from the high pressured position. He was highly paid and had a great future ahead of him. Being in a position to enjoy the finer things in life, he chose instead to pay for private medical care for his ailing mother who had a rare blood disease. Without this privileged treatment she would surely die at an early age so this commitment drove him on and gave him a real purpose in life.

The crisp snow on the moorland slopes sparkled like diamonds in the headlights as he steadily weaved his way along the narrow winding road. No street lamps and in places no road markings to help him through the dense mist to find the motorway which was still some distance away. From listening to light soothing music he tuned into the early morning news, in the slight distraction he failed to notice the ice patch stretched across the road as he encountered a bend. The crash was swift and extremely serious. He sat there hardly able to move and in total shock. His life flashed before his eyes, he was trapped as his thoughts turned to his mother. Death was inevitable as he painfully searched for his mobile to make a call; he managed to dial the number but failed to make contact. In his dazed state he tried to sum up the dire situation. If he did not get to work early he could be out of a job and no amount of Police, fire or ambulance paramedics would be able to save him from his life and death situation.

The car began to fill with smoke; the radio crackled .The institution where he worked had completely crashed making him unemployed and unable to support his mother who without the care would soon die. In the poor light he surveyed the very slight damage to his car and a thin wooden fence post, stubbed out his cigarette and continued the journey.

On arrival at work he found that his previous share dealings had soared giving him much relief. He looked for his friend and colleague to thank him for the tip off but he was nowhere to be seen. He asked the office manager who replied,

'Mr Leeson has not turned up today and his whereabouts are unknown.

THE INVISIBLE MAN

Your Honour, as the defendant in this case I have to find the prosecution evidence rather laughable and totally unacceptable. This day will be unforgettable and has made me really miserable and the outcome is debateable. The damage to my character is considerable, unbearable and very regrettable. It is inconceivable and unbelievable that someone as likeable and amicable as myself should be thought capable and responsible for this incredible and horrible chargeable crime.

On the night in question I was available and flexible as I went out in my convertible feeling excitable. The telephone number in the phone box was barely visible or readable and as she answered her voice was hardly audible. I made her a proposition which she found acceptable but the price was suddenly inflatable and I thought it advisable to be debatable. She said up front was payable if that was suitable and the contract was unbreakable. Well I thought it is going to be very pleasurable and she sounds adorable, lovable and very desirable.

I went to her accommodation just by the station and was full of ambition and anticipation as she sat in a provocative position. I had a notion she was full of emotion and there was an attraction as I made the transaction. Then suddenly she backed away without any action. I felt the tension, was this extortion or deception, maybe it was rejection in her extension as I sat with an erection but no connection. Then she grabbed my projection and made an insertion checking first there was no infection with a little inspection. I had made an exception to do without contraception and the outcome was abortion. But who's to blame there is no one name we have to share it in proportion.

You are accusing me of abandoning or abstaining and failing to be accommodating instead of abiding and addressing and agreeing to the charge. I find this amazing, agonising, alarming and annoying. I have been absorbing and answering your questioning aiming and airing my views without faulting. Yes I saw the advertising I cannot change anything but now I am admitting but I really feel you should be acquitting.

But as you cannot see that this is me the outcome is rather quizzical, so your Honour ma dear I'm out of here as I am intangible and quite invisible.

THE CHRISTENING

The flickering candles with their golden flames
shadows falling on the walls
The altar glistening on the stained glass panes
In the house of the one who softly calls.
Church bells tolling choir in place
family and friends all around
My silky gown trimmed in lace
this is my Christening on holy ground.
A man of the cloth has been appointed
to make a cross upon my face
He tells me I am now anointed
joined together in the Christian race.
Hymns are sung prayers are said
I am now a member of the faith
Gently sleeping in my bed
knowing forever I will be safe.

EXASPERATING

I went to the writing group and found it strange
To be given homework without words of a descriptive range
In every story and poem, adjective is the main word
To take them out seemed absurd
and to poets I'm sure it just never occurred

The beautiful flowers, the cloudless sky,
deep sadness and a woeful cry.
pounding heartbeats, everlasting love, must be
boring as hell without passion and frenzied ecstasy.

There must be a reason but it will blow my mind
for alternative words I am struggling to find.
Just the word flower puts thoughts in our mind
without an adjective we will never know what kind.

Take out cloudless and we are left with sky,
is it bright blue, dull grey and raining
hot and humid or full of young birds learning to fly.

This would mean April and May the time of Spring
when not only birds but people sing.
The flowers are blooming, (sorry I meant out)
and the sky, well it's the sky with stars all about
As for heartbeats, without pounding I would be dead
and not in a position for these words to be said.
Love and sadness without deep and everlasting
would leave book readers confused and grasping.

Exasperation would follow with a sigh
And they would not be woeful but just give a cry.

As for frenzied ecstasy and overpowering passion
no adjectives you would have to show compassion.
But that is the task set by John
and for me the adjectives are now long gone.
But for alternative words of any kind
This homework is understandably, horrendously,
exasperatingly, blowing my mind !!!

www.paphoswritersgroup.org

Neo's Sports Bar, Coral Bay, Cyprus

THE LODGER

One night at home while pulling up a stocking
I heard a noise at the door, someone was knocking
I clicked my sussy and tousled my hair,
opened the door, Roger the lodger was standing there

Wine in hand and wearing a smile
Would I like some company for a while
Ever so young, handsome and dapper
Why would he bother with me, an old slapper

Blonde hair so neat, teeth pearly white
boobs held high, not a bad sight.
We laughed and chatted and drank loads of wine
and everything seemed to be going fine

Then he touched my leg, stocking so smooth
kissed my lips and got in the groove
I reached for the switch and turned out the light
then passion went crazy throughout the night

He ran his fingers through my hair
but my wig came off and fell on a chair
He kissed my mouth, tongue deep beneath
and choked really hard as he pulled out my teeth

Off with a stocking, his eyes all a twinkle
till he caressed my leg now full of wrinkle
So very stiff I gently kissed his plums
and gave him a blow job with my gums

He said I think I have really been conned
By an over rated tarted up blonde
And sex is very far from being in heaven
I said, 'what do you expect, after all I am Eighty seven.'

THE LAYABOUT

I didn't really know what my purpose in life was or why I was here at all. The reason behind my being was difficult to understand. I did not do anything just lay about all day. There were a lot of close friends which was nice but none of them seemed interested in doing anything. Each morning we were disturbed as the cover was pulled off and the darkness turned to brightness as a new day began. The amount of friends was quite extensive but every so often one or two would go off into the big wide world never to be seen again. Maybe they were in need of a more interesting life and wished to travel to other countries. Who could blame them? It must be better than lazing around all day.

Sometimes I would be picked up and taken out of my home, but never went far or for very long and was soon back lying around. One day whilst out of my home with some friends I was seriously attacked and received a very nasty laceration to my side. My friends just disappeared and I never saw them again. It was a very frightening experience. I managed to return to my home but it did not feel the same as there was only one close friend left.

The weekend came, it was very quiet, we never moved at all. Monday morning was totally different the covers were off, the brightness shone through. We were picked up and forced to go our separate ways. I tried to resist but it was hopeless. A big burly man with bad breath held me tight, his grubby hand covered my face, I could not see. He pulled me towards him, the smell of tobacco was foul as he exhaled and breathed all over me. He turned me over face down, I was petrified. He began to lick my back all over, first the top then moving lower. He turned me round to face him and I waited for the final disgusting onslaught. Suddenly he pushed me onto my back over a table and held me down tight. As I resisted and tried to get up he hit me hard with his fist, I never moved again. I woke up thousands of miles from my home; I was paralysed, totally unable to move. It was at this point that I decided that if I should ever be fortunate enough to return to this world in the future, I would hope and pray that I was not a first class stamp.

STORE COMPLAINT

Dear manager, I wish to make a complaint.
I went in for milk but came out with paint.
It was inside the door, piled very high
customers were grabbing it and I heard one cry.
'This paint's so cheap, is there any blue'.
I panicked and didn't know quite what to do.
The cans were damaged and had no label,
so I asked an assistant whose name was Mabel.
The house needs painting before it goes up for sale,
I thought something neutral or pleasantly pale.
I filled two trolleys and went to the till
as I read the receipt I felt rather ill
How much does it cost to paint a house?
he will go mad, so I'll buy him a bottle of Grouse.
I took the paint home and stored it in the shed
He was at work as I lay worrying in bed
What will he do, what will he say,
about the colour, I should have bought grey
Even though it was cheap the cost was immense
Will he scream and say 'have you got no sense'
Enough is enough I could not stand the strain
so I went back to the store once again.
I spoke very nicely, not a complaint
I would like to return this load of cheap paint.
But your man on the desk said it was so cheap
a refund was out and the paint I should keep.
So I took it home and put it in the shed
thought when he comes home I am gonna be dead.

Money is tight and we feel the pinch
so please Mr, Manager, please move an inch.
Give me a refund and ease my pain
and at a later date I will come in again.
Normally I would not make a complaint
but I got over excited when I bought the paint.
The other reason I am causing a stink
Is that every can I opened was bloody bright pink!!!
Mrs Perky Pinkie, 4, Peyton Place.

DEFINITELY

Quietly spoken and with a slight limp, Pauline was not exactly a raving party animal. She had up to a couple of years ago been an extrovert enjoying the company of everyone she came into contact with. She was the life and soul of social functions but slowly all that changed and she withdrew into her own little world. Her friends tried to help and wanted to know what her problem was but she was reluctant to talk about it and distanced herself from the large circle of friends and associates she had built up over the years. Life became boring and dull plus with no interaction with others quite lonely.

Eventually she realised that her life could not continue as it was and decided to do something about it. She scoured the local newspaper advertisements and was eventually introduced to me. After she explained her problem I told her I would change her life completely and from then on we became very close. She was a young attractive woman with dark brown eyes and rich auburn hair. She had a warm endearing personality and an insatiable sex drive which I was soon to experience. We took things slowly, allowing ourselves time to get used to each other, then one day she touched me then held me tight. I began to vibrate with excitement as slowly and gently she inserted me inside her. She was tight, very tight and began to scream with joy as my senses were increased.

As the years past she began to suffer from CRAFT moments and one night she went to an elite social function leaving me at home. She was quite distraught on her return and could not understand why people had not spoken to her. She held me tight and pushed me inside her, again becoming very excited. I was aware of a strange smell and a damp sticky feeling as she shrieked and pushed me deeper. Later we went out to a hotel, she removed most of her clothes, and I lay there very still. She began to gyrate and jump up and down as I tried to stay calm inside her. We left the hotel and as we got home she had a heart attack. I told her she should not have had sex with the hotel gym instructor, all that jumping about was not good for her. She died with me inside her for the last time. I was left on my own in total despair, my existence was of no use at all without her. We had shared so many wonderful years together and now I would never experience anything like it again, for after all who in this world wants a second hand wax covered hearing aid.

Note: C.R.A.F.T (can't remember a f...... thing).

GOLDEN WEDDING ANNIVERSARY

Like the golden leaves on an Autumn day
Your wedding years have shed their way
First green and new, searching for light
Holding together night after night
Reaching for life, bonding together
Holding strong through stormy weather
Autumns come and Autumns go
But you have kept your golden glow
Fifty years as man and wife
Fifty years travelling through life
So congratulations on this very special day
Your Golden Wedding Anniversary.

A WALK THROUGH LIFE

When I was five I went to school to receive an education
To help me find my way in life towards my destination.
At aged eleven it was heaven when primary I left behind
High school's great, I found a new mate and teaching of a
different kind.

O levels next, more complex and I managed to obtain five
Grades of A arrived one day, I needed them to survive
Uni arose, my mind froze, thoughts of three years more
I got a job, earned a few bob with a company in civil law

I met a girl and with head in a whirl the two of us did wed
Had a great time, drank loads of wine and ended up in bed
At twenty five and so alive my wife was up the duff
The baby came life was never the same, yes it was tough

Another two tots wiping their bots and it was all a strain
We did our best, they flew the nest, life went on again
Years older I had to shoulder thoughts of retiring soon
With the old age pension I was feeling the tension
but the company pay-out was an absolute boon

Retired to the sun, had lots of fun, bought a three bed villa
Wined and dined and watched the occasional thriller
At eighty five, barely alive, 'what are we going to do now.
Sex was out due to the gout, computer games highbrow.
Instead we just lay in bed holding each other tight
That way we could say 'I love you darling, goodnight.'

JUSTICE

At eleven years old, Angelo Diagio dreamed of becoming a professional footballer. His whole aim in his short life was to play for his beloved country, the best football team in the world. He was already a rising star being voted the most outstanding player in his school and also the national youth team in his age group. At school he studied hard and excelled in most subjects, his homework was finished very quickly as he did not want to spend extra time studying when he could be out on the local football pitch living his dream. He wore the latest and best kit, courtesy of his parents. They were not well off and lived very modestly in a small house in a village on the outskirts of town. Angelo's older brother Fabrio, who was also a rising football star, had been killed two years ago in a motorcycle accident. The family were devastated and could not come to terms with their sad loss and as a result they focussed all their time and energy on Angelo. They both worked hard and long hours to make sure he had all the equipment and paid for the fees at the football academy. It gave them a purpose in life and helped to ease the pain of their tragic loss. Angelo did not disappoint them, he studied and played hard obtaining top grades and eventually at the age of fifteen was chosen to captain the national youth team. His future was looking very promising.

Three years later he was signed up to play for a major city club and put in the reserve team. This gave him valuable experience which he would need if he was to progress into the big time. At last he was earning some money, not a fortune but enough to be able to start paying his parents back and make life easier for them. He threw his whole mind and body into the game, determined to be the best and his efforts quickly began to show. After a few months he was called into the managers office and told that he would be playing in the first team the following Saturday. His usual position was right wing forward but to start he would be put in defence to allow him to get used to the first division atmosphere and settle in with his new team mates. He was ecstatic and rushed home to give his parents the good news. They were elated and felt so happy for him, all their care, guidance, encouragement plus financial assistance was beginning to pay off but their main pleasure was watching their beloved son making his dreams come true. His career flourished and soon he was picked to be a permanent member of the team eventually becoming the star attraction as centre forward. Due to his high goal scoring and increased moral of the side, they crept up to the top of the league table. Angelo became a celebrity, finding himself in all the national newspapers. Television interviews became a regular thing and he was always on the news broadcasts. Commercial offers began to pour in, wear this garment, use this aftershave. He found he was making lots of television adverts and the earnings from them slowly overtook his football salary. He was able to retire his parents and bought them a nice house with lovely grounds as they both enjoyed gardening. One morning having turned up for training he was told by the manager that he had been chosen to play on a regular basis for his country. Due to hard work and sheer determination Angelo's dream was now a reality but how long would it last.

A few years later, still at the height of his career playing for the national side, he began to feel that he was being taken a bit for granted. He felt that the management resented the fact that he had such a highly acclaimed career outside of football and that he was not giving a hundred percent to the club. This was nonsense as far as Angelo was concerned, having made it to the top he was determined to stay there and be the best player in the world. He no longer relied on his massive salary due to his commercial ventures but he played football and strove to be the best because he loved it. Maybe they were jealous of all his trappings and massive popularity, he did not know and he did not care, he was there to do his job to the best of his ability.

One day he was told that for the next match he would be required to step down as captain of the team.

The management suggested to the manager that it was time Angelo had a break. He was a bit confused by the request and reluctantly sat out the next game. His side managed to win one nil. He played the next game but was later requested to sit on the bench for the next two matches. The moral of the team began to fall without their star player and they soon lost games. Angelo began to question their management decisions and was told that although he was the star player they needed to build up the side in case of any future injury or sickness he may incur. He thought about it and decided it made some sense and over the next few months of being in and out of the team he felt a lot better knowing the reason for his omittence. The only problem was the team were losing too many matches and attendance figures were falling; they were in a position of losing the title of being the best in the world. Six months later Angelo had become very disillusioned with the situation and was seriously considering a move to another club. His drive in life was to play top class football and this was not happening. He was regularly asked by reporters what was going on but he found it difficult to explain. As he settled down for his tea in the five star hotel, he switched on the news. Robert Blane the chairman and president of the footballing body known as Fifa had been arrested along with some of his associates for match rigging at the highest level. Angelo sat in disbelief, he suddenly realised what had been going on with his career. Maybe soon he would be able to resume his position as captain of the best side in the world.

With his mind in turmoil and time on his hands he decided to spend a few days in the country. Setting off in his Mercedes not knowing where he would end up, just somewhere quiet and peaceful where he could relax and evaluate his life. Driving steadily along a tree lined winding road listening to the soothing music on the radio, he was startled as the 4x4 sped past him at excessive speed. He thought, you nutter , but a few seconds later it hit a log and went out of control crashing through the bushes to the right and down a steep embankment. Angelo pulled over and stood looking down; the 4x4 had come to rest upside down against a tree. He immediately leaped into action and slid down the embankment until he reached the vehicle. He recognised the driver as the vice chairman of his club, sadly he was dead. Angelo removed his body and laid him on the ground then quickly searched the vehicle. There were many bags of money possibly running into millions which he removed in case of fire. A further search revealed some tapes, diaries and ledgers which he managed to move to safety before the car burst into flames. There was nothing more he could do so he returned to his car where he read through the books. His heart began to beat faster, he found it hard to believe that the information he was holding contained details of payments received by the management of his club for match rigging by leaving him out of the side and it also included the goal keeper. Angelo was stunned, he had been brought up to be an honest person, giving his life to football and his country yet here he was at the core of corruption. He spent a few minutes wondering what to do then came to a decision. He contacted the Police informing them of the accident and that he had managed to retrieve the money. On returning to the club he made it known to the chairman and owner that he had the match rigging evidence in a safe place. Angelo lived out the rest of his career as a world celebrity footballer without any problems making all his dreams come true.

THIS LIVING WORLD

I never knew my parents
they died so I could live
They were coloured and very bright
with the happiness they could give
I was found abandoned helpless on the floor
the wind and rain beating down
could I take much more?
Lying in a soggy mire
should I have struggled and hoped?
Battered by life's elements
I was doomed and soaked.
But then a miracle of life came my way
the sun burst through and turned the
gloom into a fine spring day.
I felt energy inside so strong and fierce
I thought my skin was about to pierce
My body grew so strong and tall
never again would I fall
And as for winds and the occasional shower
It did not matter now that I was a flower!

AW

AWAY WITH THE FAIRIES.

Little Bo Peep fancied sex with a sheep
But didn't know what to do
So she made a call to someone quite small
And up popped 'Little Boy Blue
He said, 'I've no idea as i'm a bit queer
And sheep are not my call
If you want some rumpy ask Humpty Dumpty
But make sure he stays on the wall
Humpty said 'Don't do it in bed,
make sure you are on the flat'
Watch out for cows, pigs and sows
And stay clear of the odd cowpat
Now Old Mcdonald had the farm
He shouted E-I-E-I-O
This idea of yours
should be done on the moors
So I think it's time to go
But along came Mary, quite contrary
Holding a little lamb
She said to the farmer, try to stay calmer
For your views we don't give a damn
Little Bo Peep pulled on the sheep
As it bleated out Baa, Baa
How come your black as she lay on her back
Oo'h, I think you've gone too far
Snow White came next, looking perplexed
And said' iv'e brought Tom Thumb

He pushed through the crowd
and shouted out loud
Bo Peep ! I can see your bum
As the sheep reared, the farmhand appeared
'it's Whittington', cried Puss in Boots
Then Jack gave a talk
'bout the size of his stalk
But no one gave two hoots
Three bears gate-crashed
and the place was trashed
As Bo Peep let out a scream
Goldilocks had brought in the flocks
To fulfil Bo Peeps dream
After thirty or so there was no more to go
And Bo Peep was a sleeping beauty
Happy in mind
She'd been rammed from behind
As the sheep had done their duty.

FIRST TIME

It was seriously throbbing that morning, I had thought of relieving the tension myself but there was very little time left and I knew that soon I would be with her. My anxiety and tensions heightened as I fought the feelings in my body.

I suffered the thirty minute drive to where I would meet her for the first time and hopefully once I was with her all pressures I had would be released and total relief and calmness would follow.

It was my very first time and my mates had paid a lot of money for the experience. Would she deliver and give me total satisfaction. I walked up to her and eyed up her body, she was huge. Surely my mates were taking the mick. My nerves were not good, I was trembling. How could I enter that. The throbbing increased, I had to make a decision. O'h stuff it, it's paid for, I have to do it sometime and if I back out now my mates will laugh.

I gripped her tightly and forced myself inside her, the throbbing increased dramatically. Suddenly I felt a thrust so strong I thought my head was going to burst. She eased off and settled down, that was one crazy experience. I lay there for a while then suddenly she went down then up then down, I screamed with fear and excitement. I expected to explode in a dramatic ending. I took three painkillers, the throbbing in my head stopped. I lay there relaxed, happy that I had done it and with the knowledge that as I removed myself from inside her I would quite happily fly in an aeroplane again.